POSTITCH

Thank you so much for completing your journey with My Friend Stitch! I hope you had a blast coloring these pages and that Stitch filled your moments with creativity and joy.♥

If you enjoyed the book, it would be great if you left a review! It would help me so much to create more books full of magic and adventure. And if you want to share your artwork, tag me on social media – I can't wait to see your creativity in action!

Thank you again for making Stitch a part of your days. You are incredible!

Love,
Roxana B.

Made in United States
North Haven, CT
29 May 2025